KU-341-296

To Wilf Jervis-Hill K.P.

OXFORD
UNIVERSITY PRESS

Great Clarendon Street, Oxford OX2 6DP

Oxford University Press is a department of the University of
Oxford. It furthers the University's objective of excellence in
research, scholarship, and education by publishing worldwide.
Oxford is a registered trade mark of Oxford University Press in
the UK and in certain other countries

Text copyright © Oxford University Press 2009, 2010, 2011, 2018
Illustrations copyright © Korky Paul 2009, 2010, 2011, 2018
The characters in this work are the original creation of Valerie Thomas
who retains copyright in the characters.

The moral rights of the author and artist have been asserted

Database right Oxford University Press (maker)

First published as *The Misadventures of Winnie the Witch* in 2011
This edition first published in 2018

All rights reserved. No part of this publication may be
reproduced, stored in a retrieval system, or transmitted, in
any form or by any means, without the prior permission
in writing of Oxford University Press, or as expressly
permitted by law, or under terms agreed with the
appropriate reprographics rights organization. Enquiries
concerning reproduction outside the scope of the above
should be sent to the Rights Department, Oxford University
Press, at the address above.

You must not circulate this book in any other binding or cover
and you must impose this same condition on any acquirer

British Library Cataloguing in Publication Data available

ISBN: 978-0-19-276724-0 (paperback)

10 9 8 7 6 5 4 3 2 1

Printed in China

Paper used in the production of this book is a natural, recyclable
product made from wood grown in sustainable forests.
The manufacturing process conforms to the environmental
regulations of the country of origin

www.winnieandwilbur.com

Laura Owen
and Korky Paul

The Misadventures of
Winnie
the Witch

OXFORD
UNIVERSITY PRESS

Contents

WINNIE'S KNICKERS

Bump! '**Ouch!**' Swerve! '**Ow-ow-ow!**
Don't do that, Broom!' wailed Winnie.

Winnie was on her way home from shopping
for groceries, riding her broom over the treetops.
But a wiffly wind and having to dodge crows
meant that it wasn't a smooth ride.

'My bum's black and blue!' said Winnie.
'A knobbly bottom on a knobbly broomstick
is not a comfortable thing.'

She looked over her shoulder at Wilbur who
seemed perfectly happy. 'It's all right for you!' she said.

'You've got all that fur to pad you!'

Winnie went quiet as they landed. She didn't say a thing as they went into the house. Or when she dumped the shopping bags. She stood still and she stroked her chin and she said 'Hmmm' in various different tones—'Hmm, hmmm, hmmm?'

'Mrrrow?' asked Wilbur.

'I'm thinking,' said Winnie. 'Thinking of a way to save my bum from getting bruised.' She fell back into an armchair. She waggled her bottom and bounced a bit. 'That's it!' she said. 'I'll upholster my bum!'

Winnie got out her rag bag and tipped rags onto the floor.

'Hmm. I need something soft next to my skin. Ooo, feel that, Wilbur! Bunny fluff. Lovely! Then something tough to protect me from the broom knobbles. How about this?' Winnie picked up a bit of rough canvas. 'But that won't look pretty. Hmm. I do like a pretty knicker.' She pulled out all sorts of fabric and chose the prettiest.

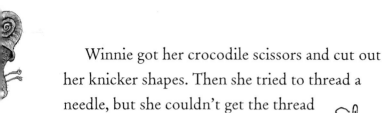

Winnie got her crocodile scissors and cut out her knicker shapes. Then she tried to thread a needle, but she couldn't get the thread through the hole.

'Blooming heck!' said Winnie. 'I need a bit of magic to help me with this. *Abracadabra!*'

In an instant there was
a squeaking and a squawking as a rat,
a toad and some fleas set to work. The fleas hopped
through the eyes of needles to thread them, while the
others stitched. Winnie clasped her hands in delight.

'Oo, I can't wait to try the knickers on!'

The knickers fitted perfectly. Wilbur put a paw
over his mouth as Winnie looked at herself in the
mirror. 'Both pretty and practical!' she said. 'Come
on, Wilbur, let's go for a test flight!'

The knickers made all the difference. Even high in
a thundercloud, with the broom swerving this way and
that, bumping up and down, Winnie sat tight.

14

'Comfy as anything!' she said. 'Not a bruise!
Er . . . are you all right, Wilbur?'

But when they got back to the house, Winnie
started wagging her finger and saying 'Hmmm' again.
'You know, Wilbur, I really am a genius. These
knickers are easy-peasy fat slug-squeezy to make
with our little helpers. Let's make more of them
and set up a knicker shop!'

So they set to work making lots of Winnie knickers.

'Put spider-web lace around the leg holes,' said Winnie. 'Then we can charge more. Now we just need a shop.' Winnie waved her wand. '*Abracadabra!*'

In an instant Winnie's front room had turned into a shop. There was a big fine till to put the money in. Winnie pressed a button on the till. **Ker-ching!** it went, and the drawer shot open, knocking Wilbur off the counter.

'Mrrrow!'

'Whoops, sorry, Wilbur, but isn't it amazing! See all those compartments for the money to go in?'

They displayed the knickers in imaginative ways and put price labels on every pair.

'Open the door, now, Wilbur, and let our customers in,' said Winnie.

Wilbur heaved the front door open.

Creeeeeak! . . . but there was nobody there.

'Oh,' said Winnie. 'Bother,' said Winnie. 'Mind you, I don't suppose anybody knows we're here. We'd better advertise. Write me a banner, Wilbur!'

Winnie's REINFORCED

Knicker♥Emporium

NOW OPEN

18

So Winnie and Wilbur flew over the
village, trailing their banner.

'Quick!' said Winnie. 'We'd better get back.
There'll be a queue outside for sure by now!'

But there wasn't a queue.

19

There was just Mrs Parmar, the school secretary.
'I could do with a pair of reinforced knickers
because I'm going ice-skating and I'm bound to fall
on my posterior from time to time, what with
being a learner,' she said.

'These knickers would be just the job for that,'
agreed Winnie. 'Now, what pattern would you care
for? Ants pants?'

'Er . . . no. I don't think so,' said Mrs Parmar.
'Have you anything plain?'

20

'We've got a lovely plain black pair with lace trim.'
'Oh, I like those!' said Mrs Parmar.
'You won't mind if the odd spider is still
working on the trim while you wear
them, will you?' said Winnie.
'Er . . .' said Mrs Parmar.
'Perhaps I . . .'

'I'll tell you what,' said Winnie. 'Since you're my first customer, Mrs P, I'll do you a deal. I'll give you a complimentary frog to gobble up the spiders once they've finished, and then you won't be bothered by tickling in your knicker region.'

'Oh dear!' said Mrs Parmar, and she turned and ran out of the door.

'Strange woman,' said Winnie. 'Botherations! I want to use my till! Is anybody else waiting for a fitting, Wilbur?'

They weren't. Nobody else came to Winnie's knicker shop all afternoon.

'I'll just have to give my knickers away,' said Winnie sadly. 'I'll send a pair to each of my sisters. That'll be a nice surprise for them.'

So Winnie parcelled up a pair of these for Wanda.

And those for Wilma.

And them for Wendy.

'**Abracadabra!**' And the parcels were on their way.

'Right,' said Winnie. 'I'll keep seven pairs for myself. One for each day of the week. But that still leaves one pair left over. What shall I do with them?' She looked towards Wilbur.

'Mrrrow!' said Wilbur, and he began to run, but Winnie had him by the tail.

'Perfect for a cat hat!' she said, shoving the knickers over Wilbur's head. 'Two holes for your ears, and ever so pretty. Is it comfortable, Wilbur?'

'Hissss!'

'Oh, well,' said Winnie. 'I have got another idea. Just let me unpack those groceries.'

Winnie tipped packets of tea into her till; a different flavour tea for each drawer. Stinkwort tea, woodlouse tea, garlic tea, nettle tea, pea tea, fish-fin tea.

'Perfect!' she said. 'Each with its own place. Now I can be creative.' She shut the drawer. 'Hmmm. Which flavour shall I try? I think stinkwort and pea.' She looked at cross Wilbur. 'With a touch of fish-fin.'

Winnie pressed the buttons.

Ker-ching!

She spooned tea into the pot and poured on boiling puddle water.

'Now watch this!' said Winnie. She pulled the spare pair of knickers over the pot.

'A hole for the spout, and another for the handle. This tea's going to keep really warm. Am I a genius, or what?'

'Hmmeow,' said Wilbur.

27

WINNIE GOES BATTY

'Mmn. Yummy in my hungry tummy!' said Winnie, licking her fingers. She was sitting on the doorstep and munching microwaved turnip chips dipped in snail sauce. To microwave a frozen chip all you had to do was wave your wand everso slightly at it and **zap!** the chips were cooked. It was very quick. 'Scrummy! Mmph!' said Winnie, stuffing lots of chips into her mouth.

Then bossy sister Wilma came round the corner.

'You do eat rubbish, Winnie!' said Wilma, looking down her long nose. 'You're always eating fast food instead of good, well-cooked home-made meals.

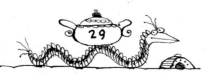

29

I don't think you look after yourself properly,
Winnie.'

'How can you call snail sauce fast?'
asked Winnie. 'Anyway, I do cook lovely fresh
food for Wilbur and for me.
If you saw what I'm
cooking for tea
tonight, then
you'd know.'

'All right, I'll come to tea and see for myself,'
said Wilma.

'Oh, heck in a hat!' said Winnie. 'Bother. Er . . .
That'll be lovely. See you later, then, Wilma. Bye!'

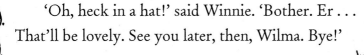

Winnie hurried into the kitchen.

'Wilbur?' she called. 'Where are you, Wilbur? You
can come out now. She's gone, but she's coming back
for tea, so we've got to cook up a feast. What shall we
give her?' Winnie looked through her recipes. 'Hmm.
I think we'll have pickled antchovies. Have we got any
pickled ants, Wilbur?'

'Meeow,' said Wilbur, pointing at a jar.

'Good. Then we'll have squid in jelly.
Is there squid in the fridge?'

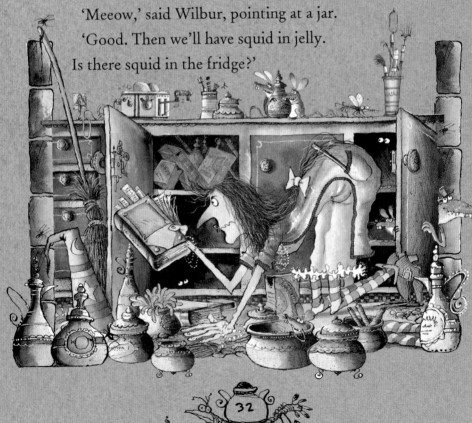

Wilbur opened the fridge door and rummaged.
'Meeow.'

'Good. Then for the main course we'll have my special batburger in a buttered bun with roasted radish relish. Look in the battery, Wilbur. Check how many

bats we've got. We might have battenberg cake for afters, so we'll need plenty of bats.'

Wilbur opened the battery door.

'Mrrow!' said Wilbur.

'Knotted noodles, you're blooming right!' said Winnie, peering in. 'There's only one diddly little bat in there!'

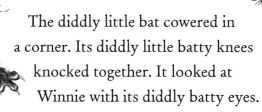

The diddly little bat cowered in
a corner. Its diddly little batty knees
knocked together. It looked at
Winnie with its diddly batty eyes.
'Mrrrow?' asked Wilbur, ready to pounce.
'Squeak!' went the diddly little bat.

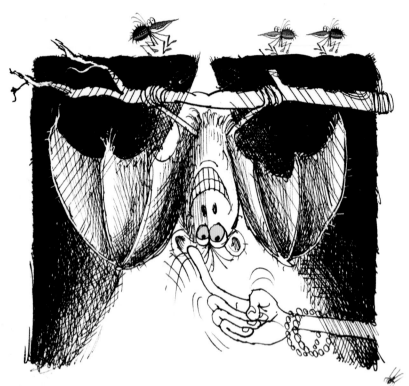

'Er . . .' said Winnie. 'No, I don't think so, Wilbur.'
She reached out a finger to stroke the soft diddly little
batty velvety head. 'This one's too scraggy-scrawny
to serve up to Wilma. Anyway, we need a whole
bagful of bats. We'd best go to the Bat Caves and get
some plump fresh ones to mash into burgers.'

So Winnie got shopping bags, and she and Wilbur
climbed onto the broom, and off they flew. But Winnie

was wriggling. **Jiggle-wiggle** went the broom.
Swerve! went the broom.

'Meeow!' protested Wilbur.

'Sorry, Wilbur,'
said Winnie.

'But there's something itching and scratching down my blooming front!' Winnie dipped her hand down the front of her dress. 'Heck and a half!'

Wobble! 'What the flipping fly-swat is this?'

Winnie pulled out something small and black
and trembling. 'It's that blooming diddly bat!'
The diddly bat trembled in her fingers. 'Ah,' said
Winnie, suddenly going soppy. 'Poor little thing!'

'Meeow!' went Wilbur.

'It just wants to go home to the Bat Cave,' said
Winnie. 'Ah, bless its diddly little heart!'
And she let the bat cling to her front
like a brooch.

'Hmph!' said Wilbur.

'Here we are!' said Winnie.

They parked the broom
outside the Bat Cave, and picked up
batting nets.

'Abracadabra!' went Winnie.

Her wand began to glow brightly, lighting
the cave, making shadows and showing bats
clinging to all the walls.

'Squeak! Squeak! Squeak!'
went the mass of bats.

'Pongy-wongy-woo!' said Winnie, holding her nose. 'These bats smell good and lively!'

Wilbur licked his lips. **Swat!** he went with his net. **Swish-swat!** went Winnie.

'Got one!' she said.

But the diddly bat scrambled up Winnie's shoulder and squeaked in her ear. **'Squeak!'**

'Oh!' said Winnie. 'That one's the diddly bat's mummy and he doesn't want her cooked into a burger.' So Winnie let that one go.

Swish-swish-swat! She caught another.

'I've got a good fat one here, Wilbur! It's as fat as a flump dumpling! Hold the wand-light so I can see it properly!' Then, 'Oh!' said Winnie, because the big fat bat was rubbing its eyes. 'This fat one's blooming well crying!' said Winnie.

'Squeak!' went the diddly bat.

'Fossilized fishcakes!' said Winnie. 'This fat one's your grandpa? Are you related to every bat in the whole blooming cave?'

'Squeak!'

Winnie put down her net. 'Oh, I give up! Come on, Wilbur. We'll have to cook something else. I'm not blooming-well eating something that's related to any friends of mine. I shall make Wilma a nice warm worm salad or something, and that'll have to do her. Come on!'

They flew back home, where they looked in the
store cupboard.

'Aha! Bottled flies,' said Winnie. 'They'll have to
do. And there's a packet of sun-dried lice too. Get out
the pans, Wilbur, she'll be here in five shakes of a
cockroach's bottom.'

Brriiiinnnnggg! Wiiiinnnniiiieeee!
went the dooryell.

'She's blooming here already! And I haven't cooked
a thing!' said Winnie.

Winnie opened the door, and there stood Wilma
with her nose in the air, sniffing.

'What can you smell?' asked Winnie, a bit worried.

'Not a thing!' said Wilma. 'You've not done any

cooking at all, have you, Winnie? I knew you
wouldn't!'

'I was going to . . .'

'Huh!' said snooty Wilma. 'Going to isn't the same
as doing. Are we to starve?'

But just then, a **sizzle** sound came from the
kitchen, and a wonderful smell curled around the
corner and up Wilma's nose.

'Oh!' she said, and she stepped into the kitchen.
'Your scraggy old cat is doing the cooking, Winnie!
Oh, and he's being helped by . . . is that a bat?'

'It is,' said Winnie. 'That's my little diddly bat.
And those are all his family!' she said, pointing around
the room where bats were all being Wilbur's little
helpers, stirring and chopping and fetching. One bat
settled like a great velvet bow in Winnie's hair.

'I see!' said Wilma. 'So what are we going to eat?
It does smell rather good!'

Winnie peered into the pans. 'Er . . . it's fly fritters
with lice sprinkles.'

'Very nice,' said Wilma.

And it was.

And when Wilma had gone, Winnie looked
around her batty room with the bats all hanging up
to sleep. 'Night-night. Mind the cats don't bite,'
said Winnie. She kissed the little diddly bat on
the nose. 'D'you know, I think I'll
join you!'

46

Winnie hung herself from the curtain pole so that she could sleep like a bat, too. And so did Wilbur, at least until he fell off. **Flump!**

WINNIE'S BUBBLE TROUBLE

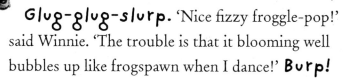

Glug-glug-slurp. 'Nice fizzy froggle-pop!' said Winnie. 'The trouble is that it blooming well bubbles up like frogspawn when I dance!' **Burp!**

Scrunch-munch-gulp. 'Meeew,' nodded Wilbur, scoffing crispy mouse tails as he waggled his hips and bopped along to the very loud Hobgoblins of Sound booming from Winnie's MP13 player.

It was a good party, even if it was just for the two of them. Even though there was no reason for the party except that they were bored. Still, Winnie and Wilbur scoffed dandelion roots in slug-nettle dip. Mouse rolls

and turnip crisps. There were balloons and streamer-weeds and party splatters.

Bang! Wheeeee! Splat!

Winnie and Wilbur went to bed very late. Wilbur went straight to sleep.

Snore, went Wilbur. **Snore-snore** pause **snore** pause. **SNORE!**

'Oh, please shush, Wilbur!' said Winnie, lumping over in bed and putting her hands over her ears.

Snore-snore-snore pause **snore** paaaauuuussseee.

SNORE-splutter!

'No!' wailed Winnie. 'I can't sleep with that noise!' She gave Wilbur a shove. Wilbur grunted and made silly noises with his lips. Then he went back to . . .

Snore-SNORE-snore pause.

Winnie put her pillow over her head, but she was wide wide awake. And she stayed wide awake for the rest of the night.

'Ooo, my head hurts! That cat is driving me as mad as a red-hot icicle!'

When the sun came up, Winnie got up too, but she was bleary-eyed. She tried to make breakfast.

Wail-wail-wail went the smoke alarm as
flames came from under the grill.

'Mrrow!' went Wilbur when she fed
him his toadstool toasty.

'Have you not heard of
"flame-grilling", you silly cat? That's
posh cooking, that is!' But Wilbur spat
the burnt toasty out and Winnie didn't fancy it either.
So they opened a can of beans and ate those instead.

Then Winnie tried to tidy up all the party mess.

Boom! The vacuum cleaner exploded.

Bang-sploosh! The washing machine erupted.

'Mrr-he-he-hee!' laughed Wilbur.

Dust and rubbish and wet clothes and soapy
slippery water went everywhere. And so did
Winnie. **Slip-crash!** into the dresser,
so that saucepans and pots fell to join
the mess. **Bang! Clang!
Smash! Crash! Ping!**
Then, **brring-brrring!**
the telling-moan began to ring.

'Dimpled slug bottoms!' wailed Winnie,
covering her ears. 'I wish I could float away from all
this in a nice calm bubble, up into the clear quiet sky.'
She reached for her wand. *Abracadabra!*
    And instantly Winnie was in a serene soapy
        see-through bubble that glinted rainbow colours
            and floated, silently and smoothly, out through
                the window and up into the sky.

'Ah,' said Winnie. She closed her eyes
and snoozed for a while as she just bubble-bobbed
on the breeze, floating up and up. When she
opened her eyes she saw birds and aeroplanes
passing, but she couldn't hear them.
'Blissaramaroodles!' said Winnie.

Then she looked down. Her house was the size of a thumbnail. Wilbur looked the size of a flea.

'Oooer!' said Winnie, trying to stand up, but she couldn't stand up in the bubble. 'I'm too blooming high in the sky! Get me down! Where's my wand?' but if Winnie waved her wand she might pop the bubble. 'Oo dear, this must be what a dilly-duckling feels like squashed inside an egg!' said Winnie, feeling a bit panicky.

'I don't want to hatch in the sky! HELP!' No sound came out of the bubble. But a small sound came within the bubble. **Parp!** 'Whoops!' said Winnie.

The bubble swelled just a little bit.

'Pongy-wongy!' said Winnie. 'Why did I eat those blooming beans for breakfast? Wilbur, save me!'

Down on the ground, Wilbur put a paw to his brow and saw Winnie's bubble, tiny and far away.

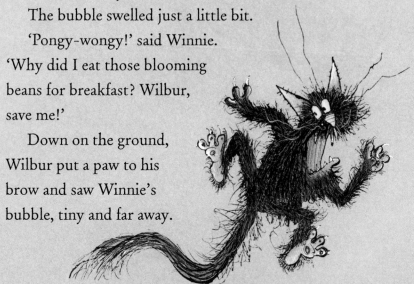

'Meeeooww!' he called, and he looked around in panic. Winnie's broom would only fly for Winnie! He hadn't got a rocket! He hadn't got wings! He couldn't catapult himself! 'Oh, meeeow!' But Wilbur did have balloons left over from the party.

'Mroww!'

Wilbur grabbed balloon strings. He tied some to
his tail and held tight to the others. Wilbur shoved
squeeeze-blop! through the door. And he began
to float up into the sky.

58

Up, up, until he was beside Winnie's bubble.
Winnie was waving and moving her mouth.

'Get me out of this pongy trouble bubble!'
mouthed Winnie.

But how could Wilbur burst her bubble without
letting her fall from the sky?

'Mrrow!' Wilbur had an idea. He let go of one
balloon.

'Wilbur!' wailed Winnie, as Wilbur and his
balloons sank beneath her. But now Wilbur's
balloons were like a cushion under Winnie's bubble.
So Winnie could pop her bubble and be safe.
She poked and poked with her wand and
pop! the bubble burst.

'Ah, fresh air!' said
Winnie. 'Whoops!' It isn't easy to
balance on a pile of balloons that are sinking
quite fast under your weight.

'Tweet tweet!'

'What the blooming . . . ?' began Winnie as a flock of big-beaky birdies flew alongside.

'A tweety-tweet treat!' went the birds, thinking that Wilbur's balloons looked like gigantic juicy grapes. So,—

Peck-pop! went one bird.
Peck-peck-pop-pop! went the others.

61

'Wiiiilllbbbuuuuurrr!' shouted
Winnie, as they sank faster and faster.
Winnie flapped her arms, trying to fly.

It didn't work, but it did remind Winnie
that she had her wand.

'Aaabbrraacaddaabbrraa!' she shouted.
Next instant Winnie and Wilbur were floating
downwards slowly and gently, holding on to a big
parachute umbrella, and . . . they landed in a lovely
grassy flowery meadow, soft and sweet smelling.

'**Tweet-tweet!**' sang some birdies.

'I don't want to hear any more from you lot!' said Winnie.

She plucked furry caterpillars from a leaf and put them into her ears as earplugs. 'Oo, they tickle!' said Winnie. 'But I don't care. I've got peace AND I'm safe on the ground!'

'Meeeow,' said Wilbur. **Yawn!**

Yawn! 'Me too!' said Winnie. So they settled down in the grass and sank into sleep. Until Wilbur began to snore.

Snore-snore pause **grunt-sniffle.**

'Not again!' wailed Winnie. But it wasn't very long before she was snoring too.

SNORE! SNORE-SNORE!
Grunt-like-a-pig **SNOOOOORE!**

So it was only the birdies who had to cover their ears.

WINNIE'S BIG CATCH

'Eh? What's this?' said Winnie, pointing to the calendar on the wall. There was a scribble round the number 13, and arrows pointing at it. Winnie put a hand over her mouth. 'Of course!' she said. 'It's your blooming birthday, isn't it, Wilbur!'

'Mew,' said Wilbur sweetly, and he fluttered his eyebrow whiskers. He rubbed his head against Winnie and looked up into her eyes.

'I've not got you a present yet!' said Winnie. 'And the thirteenth is tomorrow! But I'll get something really good, Wilbur. You stay here and comb your whiskers or something while I go into my study and do some internet shopping!'

With her lips pursed together to help her
concentrate, Winnie slowly tapped the letters
C-A-T into her computer, then clicked on
the picture of a wrapped-up present.
Up flashed pictures of cat food, cat flea
powder, cat collars, cat worm pills,
and cat litter trays.
And that was all.

    'Those are as dull as
a snail telling you about
the interior decoration of
his house! Not very
birthdayish, are
they?' said Winnie to
herself. 'And I've gone
and promised Wilbur
a really good present!'

Winnie clicked hard on the wrapped-up present picture again. Up came pictures of people doing adventurous things.

'Coo!' said Winnie. 'That's more like it! I could give
Wilbur a special day, parachuting, or waterskiing, or
sea fishing!' Winnie clapped her hands together. 'How
exciting! Which shall I choose? Oo, it's got to be
fishing. Wilbur does love his fish. Jellied squeels and
smackerel and octasquiggles, all that kind of thing.'

So Winnie clicked to book the fishing boat trip
for the next day.

Wilbur didn't sleep a wink that night, worrying that
Winnie hadn't got him anything. Winnie didn't sleep a
wink either because she was bursting with wanting to
tell Wilbur what his present was. So the moment the
cockroaches squeaked 'cockroach-a-doodle-doo!' they
both leapt out of bed.

'Happy birthday, Wilbur!' said Winnie. 'I'm taking
you on a fishing trip out to sea for your birthday!'

'Meeeow!' said Wilbur, doing a claws-up, then dancing a quick jig, sailor-style.

'Come on, then!' said Winnie. 'Let's get going!'

They flew to the harbour, and found the boat owned by Stinky Stan the fisherman. It was called THE CRABBY ROGER.

'Ahaaaa!' said Stinky Stan. 'Be you the woman and cat who think you'll be good at fishing?'

'Excuse me!' said Winnie, looking rather offended. 'Wilbur and I are both master fishermen!'

'Be you really?' said Stinky, tugging at his beard.

'Yes we do be,' said Winnie. 'So, start the engine and let's get going.'

'Mrrow?' said Wilbur.

The fishing boat was noisy and smelly. It chugged through splashy waves that got bigger and bigger.

Winnie held on to the side of the boat. Wilbur was holding tight too.

'Ha haaa!' said the fisherman. 'I knew you'd be useless at sea!'

Up and down went the boat. Up and down went Winnie's and Wilbur's tummies. Winnie had gone green. Wilbur's ears had gone flat.

'Not much of a treat so far, is it?' said Winnie.

'Blasted landlubbers!' said Stan.

'Blasted sealubber!' said Winnie.

Then the boat stopped. The sun came out, and so did the fishing rods.

'Now we'll have some fun!' said Winnie, cheering up. 'Let's catch some fish. Are you hungry, Wilbur?'

'Meeow!'

'Me too!'

'Bait yer 'ooks then,' said Stinky Stan.

Winnie and Wilbur fiddled with their hooks, attaching wriggling maggots.

'Seems a waste to feed them all to the fish!' said
Winnie, popping one in her mouth. They cast their
lines and waited . . . and waited . . . and waited.

'Hee hee,' laughed Stinky Stan, pulling up
flipping fish after flapping fish.

Then Winnie felt a tug, and wound
in her reel. 'I've got one! I've got . . .
I've got . . . er . . . a washing machine,'
she said. 'Blooming heck!'

'Meeow!'

'Oo, Wilbur, what have you got?
Reel it in! Up, up! . . . Oh dear.'
Wilbur had caught an old dustbin.

'I've got another!' shouted Winnie.

'Oh-oh! I can see it wriggling!
It's alive! It's . . . it's . . . what the heck
is one of them?' It was a very strange
creature indeed.

'I knew you'd be rubbish at fishing!' said Stinky.
'Look what I've caught!' He'd got a whole basket of
beautiful, shiny, sensible-looking fish.

'We'll eat those, then,' said Winnie.
'Not blooming likely!' said Stinky. 'Them's mine!
You catch yer own big fish!'

'All right, we will!' said Winnie. She whipped out her wand. *Abracadabra!*

And instantly, 'Mmrrrow!' said Wilbur excitedly. He'd got a bite on the end of his line.

'Hold on tight!' said Winnie, and she grabbed hold
of Wilbur as something very big tugged at the other
end. 'Heck, this one's huge!' said Winnie.

Wilbur's fish began to rise up out of the water
like a small island. It got bigger and bigger.

'It's a blooming whale!' shouted Stinky.
'Let go of your rod, cat, or it'll tip the boat over!'

But Wilbur and Winnie held on, and the boat began
to move, tugged by the whale. The boat went faster,
and faster until it was just skimming the water.

'We're waterskiing!' said Winnie. **'Yippee!'**

'Meeow!' said happy Wilbur.

The whale pulled even faster!

'Meeeeeeeeeeow!' went Wilbur
as suddenly Winnie's skirt caught
the wind and lifted them both
up into the air.
'We're parachuting!' shouted
Winnie. 'Isn't this a real
treat, Wilbur?'

'Come back!' said Stinky.

Winnie looked down and she saw how green Stinky was. 'Oh, all blooming right! *Abracadabra!*'

Instantly, the whale went, and Winnie and Wilbur floated back down onto the deck of the boat as it ran up the beach.

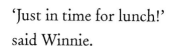

'Just in time for lunch!' said Winnie.

Winnie and Wilbur found an old oil drum to use as a barbecue. Stinky shivered and steamed beside it.

'Skewer some of those maggots onto sticks to make kebabs, Wilbur,' said Winnie. 'We can have a nice seaweed salad.' She brewed a goo stew out of the odd fishy thing and other bits and pieces.

'Er . . . I is hungry too,' said Stinky. 'But I can't fancy any of that.'

'We weren't offering you any of that,' said Winnie. 'You didn't offer us any of your fish.'

'Well,' said Stinky. 'Ahrrr. Maybe I was a bit hasty there. Um. Would you care to share me fish with Old Stinky, after all?'

'I reckon we blooming would,' said Winnie. 'You can be our guest, then it's a proper party as well as a good present! Happy birthday, Wilbur!'

CAR BOOT WINNIE

'Where's the telly remote control, Wilbur? Have you been using it to play Cats In Space again?'

'Mrrow.' Wilbur shook his head.

Winnie picked up a jam pot with mould growing out of it. She picked up a hairnet and a stinky dish slop-mop and a torn pamphlet and a cracked cup with cold puddle tea in it. She lifted up her microwave and found dust and peas, a biro, a comb, and a nest of baby spiders. She lifted up Wilbur's tail.

'**Hiss!**' went Wilbur.

'Sorry, Wilbur,' said Winnie. 'But I want to watch telly. Where is the blooming remote control?'

Winnie felt down the side of the sofa. She pulled out a dirty sock, an old biscuit, a very surprised mouse, and . . .

90

'Meeow!' said Wilbur, pointing
at Winnie's cardigan pocket.
'Oh, I'm as silly as a dizzy
flea!' said Winnie. 'Well done,
Wilbur. Sit down!'
Zap!

On came **FIND YOURSELF IN A TIDY HOUSE.**
'A tidy house leads to a tidy mind,' said the smart
presenter lady. *'Clear away your clutter! Get rid
of your rubbish!'*

'That's a good idea,' said Winnie.

'I might be able to find things if I didn't have so
much rubbish. I'm going to tidy us up!'

Winnie began picking up leaky
wellies and rusty spanners and dirty
plates and broken nail-clippers and snail-squashers
and a fork with a bent prong. 'Now, where shall I put
all this lot?' asked Winnie. 'Er . . . let me see . . . um . . .
oh. We need a good big cupboard, that's what we need.'

Winnie dropped everything on the floor.
'Come on, Wilbur,' she said. 'We're off
to the shop.'

Winnie and Wilbur **zoomed**
on her broom down to the
village furniture shop.

'I'll have that big cupboard, please,' said Winnie.

'That'll be thirteen pounds,' said the shopkeeper.

'Thirteen!' said Winnie. 'Pounds!' She pulled out her toad-skin purse. 'Er . . . will you take twenty pence? And a fluffy toffee? And an old blunder-bus ticket?'

'Thirteen pounds or nothing,' said the shopkeeper.

'OK, then!' said Winnie. 'I'll have it for nothing!'

'No you won't,' said the shopkeeper, and he began to push Winnie towards the door.

'Oh, *Abracadabra!*' said Winnie, waving her wand.

Instantly there was a crisp new note of paper money curled cosily in her purse. 'Here you are!' said Winnie, and she waved the note at the shopkeeper.

'I've never seen a note like that one before!' he said.

'It's a million-pound note,' said Winnie.

'A million pounds!!' said the shopkeeper. 'I haven't got change for that!'

'Keep the change,' said Winnie.

'Ha!' laughed the shopkeeper. 'Nobody would say "keep the change" for a real million-pound note! No, you can't fool me, Winnie the Witch. That's a forgery! Out of my shop, and don't come back until you've got some real money!' He hustled Winnie and Wilbur out through the shop door.

'That was as undignified as a rabbit with a shaved bottom!' said Winnie. 'How am I going to get enough normal money to buy that blooming cupboard?'

Wilbur pointed at a poster. It showed cars parked in a field, and lots of tables with things on, and lots of people.

'Is it one of them car boot sale thingies?' said Winnie. 'Hey, that's a blooming idea! We can sell our things! You're doing well today, Wilbur!'

So Winnie packed up her rubbish.

'Hmm. We haven't got a car, so we haven't got a car boot,' said Winnie.

'We'll have to use the broom and carry everything in bags. We can still put things in boots.'

The poor broom struggled with the weight of Winnie and Wilbur and all those boxes and boots and bags.

'Come on, Broomy!' shouted Winnie. 'Up, hup!
I'll comb your bristles for you if you can get us to the
school field!'

They landed with a **clatter-crump-crash!**

Then set up their stall on the grass. A chipped potty, a broken slug trap, a blunt snake-slitter, a torn petticoat, a bust of Great Aunt Nelly with the nose knocked off, a bowl of gloop soup.

'Our stall looks as tempting as a tortoise teacake! You hold my hat for the money, Wilbur,' said Winnie. 'We'll soon be rich!'

But—**tick-tock**—the time passed and no money went into the hat, even though there were lots

of people there. Wilbur put the hat on his head—
tick-tock—Wilbur sat on the hat—**tick-tock**—Wilbur curled up and fell asleep on the hat.

Snore-purr, snore-purr.

Winnie propped her bottom on the broom and tried not to yawn. 'Why aren't they buying anything?' said Winnie. 'Look! They're buying all sorts of rubbish from all the other stalls. That's not fair!'

But nothing on the other stalls was quite as rubbishy as the rubbish that was on Winnie's stall.

Snorrrrrre! went Winnie, and she fell off her broom-prop. **Crash! Smash!**

'Ow!' Winnie had landed on the crockery corner of her stall, sending everything flying. 'Meeow!' laughed Wilbur, waking up.

'Ha ha ha!' laughed the people at the car boot sale. They hurried over to Winnie's stall to see what was happening.

Winnie suddenly smiled. 'That's it!' she told Wilbur. 'This is our "lucky break!"'

'Mrrow?' said Wilbur.

Winnie got to her feet. **'Roll up!'** she shouted.
'Just thirteen pence to throw a boot at the stall and
see what you can smash!'

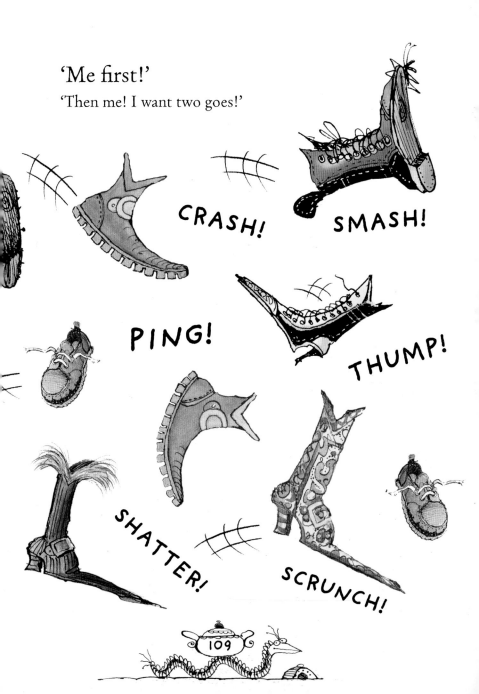

'Me first!'
'Then me! I want two goes!'

CRASH!

SMASH!

PING!

THUMP!

SHATTER!

SCRUNCH!

109

Soon Wilbur was staggering under the weight
of money in the hat.

'We don't need that cupboard any more because
we haven't got any rubbish left!' said Winnie. 'So what
shall we do with all this money? . . . Ooo, look at that!
Just what I need!'

Wilbur had his head in his paws, but Winnie was pouncing on the next stall. She'd seen a wand rack. 'Only thirteen pence? I'll have it!' And some sloth slippers. 'Ooo, I've always wanted some of them!' And a cactus cat comb.

'Mrrrow!' said Wilbur.

'Yes, I'll have that too,' said Winnie.

It didn't take long before all the money in the hat was gone. And the pile of rubbish that Winnie and Wilbur flew home with was at least as big as the pile of rubbish they'd brought in the first place.

'You know what we need, Wilbur?' said Winnie. 'We need a cupboard to put all this lot in.'

Wilbur just sighed.

BIG TOP WINNIE

'Coo, look at that!' said Winnie, giving Wilbur a nudge. 'Ooo, look at that man pretending to be a wheel! Look at that lady standing on a horse! He hee, look at the clowns! They look as silly as a hippopotamus in pigtails!'

The circus had come to the village, and everyone was there. Winnie had never seen anything like it before.

'Look, look, Wilbur!' said Winnie, flicking candyfloss in his face. 'Ha ha, see that little dog stealing the sausages!'

Then suddenly, 'Ahhh!' The whole crowd sighed, and went quiet because they were seeing something beautiful.

'Oh!' said Winnie. 'Oo, just look at that! That's as blooming lovely as a butterfly ballet, that is!' Because a lady in a sparkly bathing costume was walking high up along a rope.

The lady used an umbrella to help her balance. She threw sparkly sprinkles that winked and blinked as they fell down on to the crowd.

'Coo!' said Winnie.

Everyone in the crowd clapped and cheered. Winnie looked around at their faces, wide open and smiling.

The sparkly lady bowed, and everybody cheered.

'Hooray!' they shouted. 'Bravo!'

They whistled and they whooped and they clapped.

'Ooo, Wilbur,' said Winnie. 'I'd love it if people felt like that about me!'

114

As Winnie and Wilbur walked home, Winnie tried walking along the lines in the pavement, her arms out like an aeroplane. **Wibble-wobble, step-step.**

'See?' said Winnie. 'I'm good at this!'

Then she tried walking along a garden wall. **Wibble-wobble step-whoops!** Winnie tried to balance herself by waving one leg and two arms around. 'I'll do it along the washing line!' she told Wilbur. 'Just like that lady!'

But by the time they got home Winnie didn't just want to walk a tightrope. She wanted to put on a whole circus of her own! 'There's no point without people to see it. I'll do it for the little ordinaries at the school,' she said. 'They can cheer me and clap and say, "Ahh! Isn't she beeeeutiful!"'

'Mrrow!' said Wilbur, who didn't think that was very likely. But,

'Abracadabra!' said Winnie, and instantly poor Wilbur was in sparkly pants. 'You're my assistant,' said Winnie. 'Do a twirl!' **Twiddle-splat.** 'Try to be dignified,' said Winnie.

'Woof-he-hee!' laughed Scruff, looking through the fence from next door, where he lived with Jerry the giant.

'You can be my other assistant!' said Winnie. 'Abracadabra!'

And there was Scruff in a little sparkly waistcoat and a silly hat.

'Meeow-he-hee!'

Leap! Hiss! Pounce! Yap! They were soon chasing around the garden.

'Jerry!' called Winnie. 'Can you build me a tent, please?'

'If that's what you want, missus,' said Jerry, and he set to work.

Crash! Bang! Rip! Stitch! Heave-hup!

It wasn't long before a strange kind of big top had been made from a couple of trees, Winnie's curtains, and the tassels from her best underwear.

'*Abracadabra!*'

It had bunting and balloons and all sorts.

'Right!' said Winnie. 'Now we need to get the little ordinaries along to see my Show Of Beauty. I'll just ring Mrs Parmar.'

With the children on their way, Winnie made a few finishing touches to her big top. '*Abracadabra!*'

There was a sign for:

WINNIE'S WAND-ERFUL CIRCUS OF BEAUTIFULNESS!

'Abracadabra!'
There was a stall selling
candy moss and snotty apples.

Then the little ordinaries came marching up the path.

'Ooo!' they said when they saw the big top.

'Urgh!' they said when they saw the food.

Then the little ordinaries sat ready.

'Where's the show?' they said.

'Er . . .' said Winnie. 'Er . . . just a moment. *Abracadabra!*'

And there was Winnie in the sparkliest outfit
a circus had ever seen. **Zing!** glittered the sequins.
Twang! went the elastic where it was a bit
too tight.

'When's it going to start?' shouted the little
ordinaries.

'I just need some music, please, Jerry,' said Winnie.

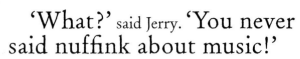

'What?' said Jerry. 'You never said nuffink about music!'

'Boo!' went the little ordinaries.

'DO something!' said Winnie, at the bottom of the ladder. So,—

'Um ti-ti, rum ti-ti,' sang Jerry. While Scruff dug-dug-dug at a drum to make a drum-roll noise and **crash!** went Wilbur with a couple of saucepan lids.

'Here I go!' said Winnie.
She climbed up to the top of the ladder,
then **wibble** stepped one toe
onto the washing line. **Wobble.**
Two feet . . .
Splat!
Winnie's slippery slippers went flying
and she fell head-first, onto her nose.
'Ha ha ha!' went the little ordinaries.

'Ouch!' said Winnie, sitting up and rubbing her bright red nose.

'He hee hee!' went the little ordinaries. 'More! More!'

'Er . . . I'll do aerobatic broom riding,' said Winnie. 'More music please, Jerry!'

'Tiddle-diddle-diddle . . . !'

Crash! Boom!

Winnie rose up on her broom. The little ordinaries had seen her flying before. Winnie went left. Winnie went right.

'Boring!' shouted the little ordinaries.

Winnie went up, then down.

'Boo!' shouted the little ordinaries.

'Watch this, then!' said Winnie. And **wibble-wobble-wibble** she carefully knelt on the broom as it flew. Then **wobble-wibble,** up onto one foot, and **wibble-wobble,** two feet. Up-up.

128

Winnie stood up. Arms out, she rode the broomstick like a scarecrow on a surfboard.

'**Ta-daa!**' went Jerry.

'Ah!' gasped the crowd.

'Is it beeeutiful?' shouted Winnie.

'Meeeeooww!' went Wilbur.

But it was too late.

Splat! went Winnie into the side of the tent, tangling like a fly in a spider's web, upside-down and high above the crowd.

'Help!' shouted Winnie.

'He hee! Ha haa!' laughed the little ordinaries. 'Winnie's so funny!'

Jerry stepped forward and lifted Winnie down. '**You can wear my shoes if you want, missus!**' said Jerry, so Winnie put on Jerry's shoes. They were enormous.

'Ha ha!' went the little ordinaries. 'Winnie's a clown!'

'What?' said Winnie. But with her red nose and
the big shoes, she did look like a clown. And as
soon as she tried to walk **trip-bang!** she fell over
Scruff and into a bucket of water.

'Stupid blooming dog!' shouted Winnie.

'Ha ha haa!'

Winnie picked up another bucket of water
and began to run after Scruff, and Wilbur
chased after Winnie, and Jerry
chased after Wilbur.

132

'Hooray!' shouted the crowd as Scruff and Winnie and Wilbur and Jerry fell **bump-bump-bump-bump!** into the sawdust.

Winnie sat up. She heard cheering and clapping and love.

'They blooming like us now that we're silly!' she said. 'Come on, Wilbur! Chase me up the ladder!' So off they went, chasing and falling and pushing and being daft.

'He hee, ho, ha!'

'Thank you, Winnie!' said Mrs Parmar.

'You were so funny, Winnie!' said the little ordinaries. 'We love you!'

'Really truly?' said Winnie. And she got out a huge spotty hankie and blew her nose on it. **Snort!** 'Who needs beauty when you can laugh, eh, Wilbur?'

133

WINNIE SCORES!

Winnie and Wilbur were waiting to watch a football
match at the village school.

'Meeow?' Wilbur pointed a claw at Winnie's basket.

'Oh, just a few snackaroos to keep us going,'
said Winnie. 'I've brought pickled toad eggs, your
favourite turkey tonsil tit-bits and a few sugared
slow-worm tongues.'

Wilbur licked his lips.

'And I've brought . . .' went on Winnie.

But a small boy called Sam was tugging at her
sleeve. Sam pointed at Winnie's legs. 'You've got
football socks on,' he said.

'They're not socks, they're stockings,' said Winnie. 'And they're nothing to do with football.'

'They're just like mine, so you must be in our team!' said Sam.

'I don't know how to play f—' began Winnie, but Sam wasn't listening. He was hauling her over to where the players were standing.

'See that other team?' said Sam. He pointed to
the ones wearing purple and green. 'They're the
Boggle-End Rovers.' Sam pointed to the biggest girl.

'That one's Big Doris. She's their captain. That's
why we need a big girl too. We need you, Winnie.'

Winnie rolled up her sleeves. 'Righto,' she said.
'You just tell me how to play the game, and I'll do it.'

'Well, you must get the ball into the net to score,'
said Sam.

'Easy-peasy, fat-slug squeezy!' said Winnie.
She took out her wand. *Abracadabra!*

The ball shot from Sam's hands and into the net.

'Hooray!' said Winnie. 'We win!'

'No!' said Sam. 'You can't start until the whistle's
blown!'

'Blooming heck,' said Winnie.

138

'Give me better instructions, Sam!
What whistle? Let's get started!
Come on, my little ordinaries!'

Brrrrip! went the whistle, and instantly Big
Doris was kicking the ball, elbowing a boy, and
stamping on Winnie's toes, all at the same time.

'Oooo, me bunions!' shrieked Winnie, hopping
on one leg and clutching her ankle. 'You mouldy little
cheat!' she shouted at Doris. But the Rovers had the
ball and were passing it from one to another, zig-
zagging towards where Sam stood in goal, his knees
knocking together.

Pow! went the ball.

Leap! went Sam in the wrong direction.

Zap! went the ball, straight into the net.

'Goal!' shouted Doris.

Brrrrip! went the whistle, and they were off again. **Thump, trip, hit.**

'Ow, ow, ow!' went Winnie's team.

Kick, kick! went the Rovers.

'Goal! Ner-ner, we're the best. Their big captain's got a hairy chest! Two-nil to the Rovers! Eas-sey! Eas-sey!'

'Oh, kangaroos' poos!' said Winnie. 'Where's my wand, Wilbur? *Abracadabra!*'

Instantly the elastic was gone from the top of all the Boggle-End Rovers' shorts. And there was one long elastic between Winnie's leg and the ball.

Now Winnie was off down the field, kicking the ball. And every time a Rover, clutching his or her shorts, tried to reach the ball—**boing!**—the ball bounced straight back to Winnie's foot.

Kick-boing! Kick-boing! Winnie was charging along, heading for goal. The village was cheering, 'Win-nie! Win-nie!'

143

Kick-boing, kick-boing went Winnie,
nearer and nearer to the goal.

'You're the stinky cheat!' shouted Doris to Winnie.
'Ref! Ref! She's got the ball on elastic!'

But Mrs Parmar took no notice. Winnie was in front of the goal. She swung back her leg to give a mighty **KICK!** The ball zapped straight towards the goal.

'Yes!' shouted the village . . .

. . . but just as the ball was about to cross the line.

BOING! it turned and THUNK! it hit Winnie right on her forehead, knocking her flat on her back.

'Mrrreeeow!' Wilbur rushed onto the pitch. 'Mrrow?'

'I'm seeing stars!' said Winnie in a dreamy voice. 'Stars and moons and rockets . . .'

The Rovers had the ball now.

'. . . and aliens and comets and . . .' went on Winnie.

Doris was heading towards the goal. She ran past Wilbur and Winnie.

'. . . green monsters and galaxies . . .' said Winnie.

'Silly old witch!' shouted Doris. 'Smelly old cat!'

'WHAT?!' shouted Winnie, suddenly awake and sitting up. 'What did you say about my Wilbur?!'

Winnie was up on her feet. She ran fast and she ran true. **Kick!** She kicked the ball away from Doris.

She swung her leg back and gave the biggest **KICK**
of her life and . . . zapped the ball straight into the net!

'Goal!' shouted Winnie. She pulled her dress over
her head and ran around the field. But only the Rovers
were cheering.

Winnie put down her dress. She saw Wilbur
shaking his head.

'But I scored!' said Winnie.

'You scored it for the wrong team!' said Sam.

'Boo!' went the children.

'Boo who?' said Winnie. 'Me? Then I'll go and
see to the refreshments. At least I can get that right!'

So Winnie set out her special snackaroos.

Brrrrip! went Mrs Parmar's whistle. 'Half time!'
The Boggle-End Rovers got to the food first. The
village children didn't seem to mind. Doris grabbed
handfuls of the little scab patties. She dipped them
into the mildew, then stuffed them into her mouth.

'Yuck!' she said. **Spit!** 'Euch!'

'What? Don't you like them?' asked Winnie.
'Have a nice dribble smoothie to wash them down.'

Slurp! 'Euch!'

Now all the Rovers were clutching their
tummies.

Brrrrip! went Mrs Parmar's whistle. 'Second half! Erm . . . Winnie, please could you put the elastic back into their shorts?'

'S'pose so,' said Winnie. *'Abracadabra!'*

The two teams got ready to play.

'Don't worry if you lose, my little ordinaries!' shouted Winnie to the village team. 'I promise I'll cook a special tea for the losers!'

Sam looked at his team. 'We've GOT to win!'

Kick, dribble, dodge, kick!

'Goal!' the village school team scored, and again and again and again.

'Four all!' shouted Mrs Parmar.

'Tea for all the players if you draw!' said Winnie.

'Come on!' shouted Sam to his team. He darted under the leg of Big Doris, sneaked the ball sideways, ran forward, and ... **pow!** he kicked the ball into goal so hard that it bulged the net and bounced back to hit Doris on the bum.

Brrrrip! went the whistle.
The game was over.

'Yay!' shouted the village.

'Hooray!' shouted Winnie.
But she told Sam, 'I did promise
my tea to the losing side,
so I'm afraid it will all
have to be for the Rovers.'

'That's OK,' said Sam.
'Do you know, Winnie,
you're as good at
football as you are
at cooking!'

'Am I?' said Winnie.
'Ooo, what a lovely
thing to say, Sam.'

153

WINNIE DIGS DEEP

'Phewy-dewy, Wilbur, I'm as hot as a
hot dog with ten hot-water bottles!'
said Winnie. She emptied a jug of water
over her head, and it steamed.

Tttttttsssssssssss!

'Meow.' Wilbur was wilting
in the heat too.

'This sunshine is going to melt us,'
said Winnie. 'I'll soon be just a
blooming pile of clothes on the
pavement, and you'll just be a bit
of black fluff and whiskers. Where
can we find some shade?'

There was one place in the village that was always cool, and that was the museum. It had high ceilings and stone walls and it echoed.

'Ahhhh!' sighed Winnie.

Ahhhh! went the walls.

'Shushshsh!' said the attendant.

Shushshsh! went the walls.

So Winnie and Wilbur wandered around the museum, looking at dinosaur bones.

'Scruff from next door would like to chew on that one!' said Winnie.

'Shush!' said the attendant.

Shush! went the walls.

Winnie and Wilbur looked at glass cases full of dead insects and stuffed animals.

'That ugly one looks just like you!' said Winnie to Wilbur. 'Oh, it is you!' Because the glass case worked like a mirror. 'He hee, ha haa!'

He hee, ha haa went the walls.

'Shushsh!'

Shushsh!

'What else is there?' said Winnie.

There were cabinets full of cracked pots and bits of rusty metal pins and brooches and dirty bent old coins. Winnie wrinkled her nose.

'They're not very pretty! Why are they there?'

'Because,' said the attendant, wagging a finger, 'they is treasure and they is worth a very great deal of money! Now please shush, Modom, and please take that h'animal out of here. Such h'animals is not allowed in museums h'except when they is in a glass case, clearly labelled.'

'That's a silly rule!' said Winnie.

But she and Wilbur went back out into the sunshine.

'Meeeow?' asked Wilbur.

'We're going home to dig up our own treasure!' said Winnie. 'We can make a museum of our own!'

Winnie looked at her garden.

'Er . . . where shall we begin digging? Oo, I know!' Winnie waved her wand.

'Abracadabra!'

Instantly Winnie had a metal detector in her hand.

Buzz it went. **Buzz-buzz-squeal!**

'Oo!' said Winnie. 'It's found something already! Dig just there, Wilbur!'

So Wilbur dug.

'Mrrow!' he said crossly. Digging is hot work when you are wearing a fur coat.

Dig-throw, dig-throw went Wilbur.

'Just a blooming button!' complained Winnie.

Squeeeaaa!

insisted the metal
detector.

'Keep digging!'
said Winnie.

And suddenly Wilbur's paw hit
something.

'Ooo, what is it?' asked Winnie,
jumping up and down. 'Let me see!
Oh! A rusty old cat food tin.
Knitted blooming noodles, Wilbur! Let's try again.'

Buzz-buzz-buzz-squeal!

'What we need is someone who's really good at
digging. Go and fetch Scruff!'

Wilbur dug. Winnie dug. Scruff came over from
next door and he dug-dug-dug. Then Jerry came over
with his giant spade and he DUG.

'Wow!' said Winnie as earth flew everywhere,
and so did 'treasures'. There were old nails,
a hair grip, a bent fork and some dentures.

'There must be some real treasure somewhere,' said Winnie. 'Dig a bit deeper, please, Jerry.'

'OK, missus,' said Jerry, and he dug and dug, digging up cables and pipes and bones.

'Ruff!' went Scruff.

'This is hot work!' said Jerry, so Winnie brought out a big jug of seaweed squash for them all.

166

'Er . . . I fink I'll give that a miss, missus,' said Jerry, and he went on digging.

DIG-DIG. As he dug, Jerry sank lower and lower until all that you could see was his curly hair level with the grass. A mountain of soil and bricks and roots was growing beside the hole.

'Have you found anything good yet?' asked Winnie.

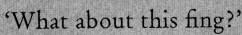

'What about this fing?'

Jerry handed up something
round and metal and . . .

'Ooo!' said Winnie.
'It's a Viking helmet! Lost
by a brave Viking who . . .
Oh. Er . . . I think maybe it's just my
old cauldron. Try again, Jerry!'

Bleep-beeep-squeal!

'Try just down there!'

As the afternoon wore on, the hole got bigger,
the soil mountain got bigger, and Winnie and
Jerry and Wilbur and Scruff got hotter and
tireder and crosser.

The pile of found things got
higher, but none of them
looked to Winnie as though
they would be
worth 'the great deal
of money' that the
museum treasures were.

'You might like these!' said Jerry, and he held up something small and wriggly with lots of legs and eyes and tails and ears.

'Coo!' said Winnie. 'That's a brand new kind of bug! It looks yummy! Are there more of them, Jerry?'

'There's all sorts,' said Jerry.

So Winnie went down on a rope to the bottom
of the hole and she filled up a bucket with
deep-soil bugs.

It was trickier getting back up with a bucketful
of bugs.

'All yummy scrummy in my tummy!' said Winnie.
'Oo, I wonder if the museum would like to label some
of them and put them in a cabinet? I'll give that man
a moan call and see if he's interested.'

'Does you want me to go on
digging?' asked Jerry.

'Just one more dig for luck, please, Jerry,' said
Winnie. 'Then I'll get you a bowl of pickle ice cream.'

So . . .

Dig went Jerry, and suddenly . . .

Whooosh! . . . water came gushing into the hole
and up floated Jerry.

'Ah! That's nice!'

'Ruff-ruff!' barked Scruff, all excited. He leapt into
the water and doggy-paddled round in circles.

'We've got our own blooming swimming pool!' said Winnie. 'Come on, Wilbur! Dive in!'

'Abracadabra!' went Winnie, and instantly there was a slide down the pile of diggings into the pool. **Wheee-splosh!** went Scruff and Wilbur.

Along came the museum attendant. He looked at the pile of findings. 'Modom, is you thinking of selling those h'objects?'

'Oh, that lot!' said Winnie. 'You can have it for nothing.

Just put all our names on the label in your display.
After all, we are the treasure seekers what found it.'

The four treasure seekers spent all afternoon in
their pool then Jerry and Scruff went home.

'You know what, Wilbur? Good friends are better
blooming treasure than rusty old pins!' said Winnie.

Don't forget to visit:

www.winnieandwilbur.com